The Cool Chick's Guide to BaseBaLL

The Cool Chick's Guide to Baseball

Lisa Martin

Illustrated by Sheryl Dickert

Gibbs Smith, Publisher
Salt Lake City

First Edition
07 06 05 04 03   5 4 3 2 1

Published by
Gibbs Smith, Publisher
P.O. Box 667
Layton, Utah 84041

Orders: (1-800) 748-5439
www.gibbs-smith.com

Edited by Jennifer Adams
Designed by Sheryl Dickert
Printed and bound in the United States of America

Library of Congress Cataloging-in-Publication Data

Martin, Lisa.
The cool chick's guide to baseball / by Lisa Martin.-- 1st ed.
p. cm.
ISBN 1-58685-259-0
1. Baseball. 2. Baseball--Terminology. I. Title.
GV867 .M32 2003
796.357--dc21
2002152109

Contents

ACKNOWLEDGMENTS

For Chuck, an even better husband than fan of the Mets.

And with special thanks to the following cool chicks:

Jennifer Adams, Elise Anthony, Madge Baird, Sheree Bykofsky, Sheryl Dickert, Cinda Lack, Betty Lou Phillips, Janet Rosen, Deborah Takahara, Jill Vollmer, those wonderful wacky Notman women, chicklet Paige, and the coolest of the coolest—my mom.

Thanks, also, to a few fine fellows: Terry Cagle (Rangers), Ian McGaughey (Yankees), Jack Schnedler (Cardinals), David Wells (Padres), and my dad, who knows a thing or two about everything.

Introduction

Baseball is like shopping.

The serious shopper devotes endless hours to perusing racks, browsing through bins, and scrutinizing sale merchandise, all in a quest for one thrilling moment of discovery: stumbling upon a sensational pair of jeans half-off or a superb shoe that fits like Cinderella's glass slipper or some such fabulous find.

The resulting ecstasy easily overshadows all of the preceding tedium. And therein lies the most compelling argument in favor of The Great Game: sure, baseball has its less-than-spellbinding stretches, but the aficionado lives for the fleeting exhilaration of a triple play or a grand slam or a game-ending strikeout with the bases loaded.

That said, I still prefer stalking the perfect little black dress to sitting in front of the TV while the baseball buffs in my life argue with the umpires, slam the opposing team, and lecture on the subtleties of the strike zone. But at least these days I can actually enjoy the occasional inning. The source of this new peace with my mate's passion? I learned a bit about the game.

In the spirit of that discovery, I wrote *The Cool Chick's Guide to Baseball*. My goal in writing this guidebook is to give other nonfans enough information to make them comfortable with the game. I aim to answer the questions a casual viewer may feel somewhat self-conscious asking. With an understanding of the basics, as well as a look at other essential issues (wardrobe hits and errors; calorie counts of ballpark fare; and so on), perhaps then you too will find the National Pastime a modest pleasure rather than a punishment.

Absorb this guide in a single sitting or use it for reference during play. However it fits into your life, I can promise you this: knowledge is cool.

And so is she who seeks it.

Lisa

CHAPTER 1

Playing the Field: Who, What, and Where

No one expects this diamond to become your best friend. But if you're after a better grasp of the game, the ballpark is the place to begin.

The entire playing field is known as the **diamond**. At the heart of the diamond is the dirt and grass **infield**. It's laid out with **first**, **second**, and **third base**, each ninety feet apart and marked by poofy white canvas squares called bags. Dirt lanes or base paths connect the three bases and lead to **home plate**. The plate itself is a rubber mat that sits flush with the ground and looks like the outline of a crosswalk sign or a house, with the roof pointing at the catcher.

Whether played on the grass inside a multimillion-dollar stadium or on the asphalt of a neighborhood cul-de-sac, the basic premise of baseball remains the same: the nine players on the team at bat try to hit the ball, run the bases, and touch home plate to score. The other team's nine players (the guys in the field when their opponents are hitting) work to foil the batter and runners. The teams take turns playing offense and defense, and at the end of nine innings, the team with the most runs wins. (In baseball say "runs"; never say "points.")

An inning consists of six outs—the first three for the visiting team, the second three for the home team. Games have a minimum of nine innings. In the case of a tie, the game goes longer (i.e., heads into extra innings) to determine a winner.

The chalked-out rectangle on either side of home plate is the **batter's box**; hitters must stand inside this area while swinging. Behind the batter, with a view of all the on-field action, is the catcher. He spends most of the game crouching in the **catcher's box**, another area designated by white chalk.

The **strike zone** is an all-important area that has no visible borders. It is defined as the area between the hitter's knees and the letters on the front of his uniform, the width of home plate. To count as a strike, the ball must be thrown through this invisible space. Umpires rule anything that misses the strike zone a "ball." More on this in Chapter 2.

If a batter accumulates three strikes, he's out. The only exception is a foul ball, which is a batted ball that lands beyond the white foul lines. Foul balls cannot count as the third strike unless they're a bunt (more on bunts in Chapter 2). That means the hitter can foul off an unlimited number of balls. And believe me, some batters spend an eternity sending those babies into the stands.

While one player is at bat, the next guy in the lineup stands inside one of two **on-deck circles**, an area several yards behind and to the left or right of the plate. He often warms up there as the teammate who precedes him in the batting order faces the pitcher.

The **pitcher's mound**, a mass of dirt elevated almost a foot above the rest of the field, is sixty feet, six inches away from home plate—that's the equivalent of six convertible coupes bumper to bumper. From his windup until he releases the ball, the pitcher must keep at least one foot on the rubber mat (often simply called "the rubber") that sits smack in the center of the mound.

The pitcher's mound is part of the infield, which also includes the curved strip of dirt just beyond the bases. The **outfield** starts where the grass resumes and goes all the way to the back wall or fence. The outfield in every big-league ballpark has a different size and shape. That means some players have an easier time hitting home runs in certain stadiums than others. Major League Baseball does specify that home plate must be no less than 325 feet from the closest outfield fence, though that's not the case in several of the oldest stadiums.

Some say the entire baseball field looks like the side view of a diamond solitaire, but to me it more closely resembles a generous slice of pizza, almost a quarter of the pie. Consider the crust the outer walls, while the pointy part is the area around home plate. The side edges translate into the two **foul lines** or baselines. Both foul lines are marked in white chalk and radiate from home plate, run past first and third bases respectively, and continue to the outer walls. Any ball fouled into the stands is out of play.

While members of the team batting wait their turn at the plate, they loiter and lounge (and sometimes spit) in what's known as the **dugout**. The manager and coaches stay there throughout the game; the dugout also houses the club's equipment. Typically, the home team's dugout sits along the first-base line; the visitor's dugout is beside the third-base line.

The **bullpen** is a long narrow area on one side of the field or beyond the outfield fence or wall. During the game, up to seven relief pitchers warm up on the two mounds in the bullpen by throwing to a bullpen catcher.

So, just to review, some of the terminology you should know by this point includes infield, outfield, home plate, batter's box, catcher's box, strike zone, on-deck circles, pitcher's mound, foul lines, dugout, and bullpen. Not bad for a beginner!

When playing defense, nine members of a ball club position themselves at various points around the field: pitcher, catcher, first baseman, second baseman, third baseman, shortstop, left fielder, center fielder, and right fielder. The shortstop, and first, second, and third basemen are also called **infielders**. The left fielder, center fielder, and right fielder are known as **outfielders**. The pitcher and catcher are, well, the pitcher and catcher.

What do these players do? The **pitcher** is the prince of the ballpark, controlling not only the pace of the game but often its outcome. Chapter 4 is all about pitchers and the balls they throw.

Though the pitcher grabs most of the glory, it's the guy on the other end of the ball who has the most physically demanding duty on the field. The **catcher** squats for hours on end, ready to receive 150 or so pitches per game. He also tags out baserunners trying to score, often using his buffed-up body to block the way. A catcher can take hard hits in more ways than one: it's no wonder he wears a thick leather mitt, plenty of protective padding, and a mask.

The catcher is the single most important player in terms of defense. Throughout the game, he tells his pitcher what to throw via a series of crotch-level hand signs. For example, one finger pointing to the ground is for a fastball, two down equals a curveball, wiggling all of the fingers signals a change-up, and so on.

The **first baseman** is the only infielder likely to be a lefty. Since first base sits in the right corner of the diamond, more often than not the ball winds up on his right. And, conveniently, that's where a lefthander wears his mitt, making it easier for him to catch the ball with his right hand. That leaves his dominant hand free for throwing.

The guy manning second base doesn't need the most powerful arm but he's got to keep his eye on the ball: in the course of his career, countless ground balls zoom past the pitcher and into the **second baseman**'s territory, the area between first and second base. He also must cover second base and throw accurately to first and third.

Third basemen often find themselves lobbing balls all the way to first; it's no wonder most have bulging biceps. They field ground balls and line drives hit down the third baseline. Third base is called the hot corner, not because of the baseman's smoldering good looks, but because a lot of the action is there, as the defense tries to tag out runners before they reach home plate and score.

Widely considered among the best athletes in the park, **shortstops** find themselves in charge of more acreage than any other infielder. From their spot between second and third base, they veer to the left and right in order to field screaming grounders and to make long, accurate, and sometimes acrobatic throws to first. The best of the bunch make big bucks for their efforts. The Rangers' Alex Rodriguez (a.k.a. A-Rod), for example, will haul in around $114,000 *per game* for years to come. There are 162 games in a major-league season, so you do the math.

Two of the three outfielders—the **center fielder** and **right fielder**—have arms conditioned for long throws. **Left fielders**, however, are thought to play one of the easiest of all positions. Though a lot of fly balls come their way, when they have to turn around and throw, it's usually to nearby second or third base. Managers often hide a "weak arm" in left field.

So now you know a bit about the positions the fielders play. But there are still a few good men you need to meet.

From the first inning to the last, the only guys always on the field are the **umpires**. At each regular season game, four umps situate themselves around the bases. One squats behind the catcher at home plate; the others are stationed near first, second, and third. Chapter 5 is devoted to baseball's ultimate arbiters.

Also around the stadium on game day are the manager, coaches, trainers, and scorers.

The **manager** is the brains of the operation, the top coach who has final say in matters relating to his team. He determines who on his 25-man roster will play that day. He also sets the batting order before the first pitch. Managers motivate the players, select strategies, and adjust lineups throughout the game. Often former players themselves, managers are frequently type-A guys who live to win. And it shows: their on-field antics, especially when they become upset with the umpire, can be downright entertaining.

If the manager serves as a field general, then among the key weapons in his arsenal is the **sign**. He communicates with his players and coaching staff using a series of funky motions and movements almost as old as baseball itself. Every club—from T-ball tots to the pros—employs the same set of hand signals: pulling an ear, tapping the nose, clapping hands, and so on. To prevent opponents from understanding these nonverbal instructions, teams use what's known as an **indicator sign**.

The indicator sign, which is decided on before each

game, can be anything from touching the bill of a cap to tapping the nose. During play, a manager, coach, or player may cross himself, tap his chest, or do any number of gyrations that are meaningless until he gives the indicator sign, say tugging his left ear. The very next sign is the one he wants his players to follow. So now when you see players doing those strange-looking signals, you know what it's all about.

While his team is batting, two of the manager's lieutenants, the **first base coach** and **third base coach**, are on the field. They should (but often don't) stand inside the chalked-out coaches boxes near those bases in foul territory. They don't do much beyond telling the baserunners when to haul you-know-what and when to stay put. Of the two, the third base coach has the greater responsibility, since he decides when a player should try to score.

Every club has a **pitching coach** and a **bullpen coach**, both of whom work with pitchers on mechanics and delivery, help keep them in good shape between starts (i.e., games played), and counsel them on how to pitch to various players in the opponent's lineup. The pitching coach is with the manager in the dugout during the games. The bullpen coach is in the bullpen with the relief pitchers.

Hitting instructors work with batters on swings, stances, and tactics. These coaches also find themselves serving as amateur shrinks, giving guidance and imparting wisdom to slumping players.

Before the game, the **bench coaches** (often the manager's best buddies) study the opposing team's batters to anticipate where on the field they think a particular player will hit the ball. Those predictions help these coaches determine where their fielders should stand. One bench coach works with the infielders; the other oversees the outfielders.

Also congregating in the dugout on game days are the **trainers**, the men who help keep the players healthy and fit. Today's trainers do more than stick a pitcher's elbow in a bucket of ice. Most of them have degrees in sports medicine and are experts on fitness and exercise.

If you love courting controversy, you'd undoubtedly bond with the game's official **scorer**. Local sportswriters usually fill this rotating position, but anyone aspiring to score a game needs skin thicker than a rhino's. Sitting in the press box, which is behind home plate and up a level, the scorer determines whether a particular batted ball is a hit or an error. If a fielder should have made a simple play—like catching a fly ball or throwing a short distance to first base—but did not, it counts as an error. Otherwise, it's a hit.

Like the ump's, the official scorer's word is law: his rulings not only appear within seconds on the stadium scoreboard and on TV screens coast to coast, they're also logged into the history books. Also like the ump, scorers are often subjected to intense criticism by managers, players, and fans. Not surprisingly, a fielder can become irate if he believes he was unfairly charged with an error. And some players don't exactly suffer in silence if they feel they've been wronged.

Cool: Lock the number nine into your mind. That's how many guys play the field at one time: the pitcher, catcher, first baseman, second baseman, third baseman, shortstop, left fielder, center fielder, and right fielder.

Cooler: Conveniently, nine is also the number of innings in a game. Tie scores take the games to extra innings.

Coolest: The manager is the head of the team's coaching

staff. But never call him "coach"—that's for football and basketball.

CHAPTER 2

Looking to Score:
The Rules of Offense

The national anthem has blared over the sound system. The umps and the fielders are poised at various points around the diamond. Were this the movies, someone would yell, "Action!" But in baseball, the home plate umpire bellows, "Play ball!"

Before the game begins, however, the manager must establish the order in which his players will hit. The sequence is called the **lineup** or **batting order**.

The game really gets going when the first batter, dubbed the **leadoff hitter**, steps up to the plate. His goal is simple: make it to first base before the ball does. The leadoff man needs to be a reliable contact hitter, consistently "slapping the ball around" in fair territory. It also helps if he runs like the wind. In fact, the minute any batter hits the ball, he becomes known as the runner; it's a big-time blunder to say, "a batter's on base."

No one expects, or even especially wants, the leadoff hitter to hit home runs. Instead, the manager needs him on base, where he can pester the pitcher. Annoying as a fly buzzing around a party of picnickers, the leadoff man tries to distract the pitcher by threatening to **steal a base** (that is, sprint to the next base and touch the bag before someone can tag him or successfully throw the ball to the baseman).

Like the leadoff batter, the second man in the lineup is a "table setter," a dependable hitter who gets on base so the musclemen who follow can drive him home. Often, the second batter in the lineup is also a speed demon with a penchant for stealing bases.

Ball clubs count on the third, fourth, fifth, and even sixth batters to drive in runs or, in other words, to hit the ball hard enough and far enough that the runners on base can make it to home plate and score. That's the main reason the power hitters (also called the "big bats" and "sluggers") are put there in the lineup. The fourth-place guy is especially important. He's called the "cleanup hitter" because it's his job to "clean the bases" of runners. Managers look to these guys to score and to make it possible for their teammates to do the same. As a group, the third through sixth batters are known as the "heart of the lineup"—maybe because everyone loves a good hitter.

Though this assessment may rankle many a seventh, eighth, and ninth man in the lineup, players are parked in those slots because they're generally the least successful or most inconsistent batters on the team. In the National League, the pitcher almost always hits ninth. In the American League, the pitcher never bats. (Note: Major League Baseball has two leagues—the National League and the American League. Chapter 6 has more details.)

Why don't pitchers hit in the American League? It's because there's a position unique to that league called the **designated hitter**. This guy's only job is to hit in place of the pitcher. The designated hitter may bat anywhere in his team's lineup. When National League and American League clubs go head-to-head, the designated hitter plays only in American League ballparks, never in National League ballparks. If that sounds weird—well, it is.

Say a runner makes it to second base. He is now in what's known as **scoring position**. (This has nothing to do with dating.) On a base hit (any hit that enables the batter to reach base safely), many of these pro athletes can run the roughly 180 feet from second base to home plate faster than an outfielder can get the ball to the catcher.

Let's say the third batter in the lineup makes it to first base, advancing the "table setters" to second and third.

Now the **bases are loaded** (or the "bases are juiced," the "bases are drunk," even "the sacks are jammed"). If the fourth batter (the cleanup hitter) hits a home run, it's the ultimate offensive play. It's called a **grand slam**, driving in four runs. But even if the batter simply hits a ground ball, odds are that the runner on third will make it to home plate and score.

Every batter's nemesis is the strike. The umpire calls a **strike** when the batter swings at—but misses—a ball or when he fouls off a ball (meaning hits a ball that lands in foul territory before anyone catches it). The ump also calls a strike when a pitch sails through the strike zone but the batter doesn't swing.

If a pitch isn't a strike, it's a **ball**. A ball is any pitch that misses the strike zone: it's too high or low, or outside that imaginary area. If four balls are thrown to a batter, he walks to first base; in other words, because the pitcher threw four balls instead of three strikes, the guy at bat advances to first

base without a hit. **Walks** are a real headache to managers, pitching coaches, and, of course, the pitchers.

The combination of balls and strikes a player accumulates while at the plate is known as the **count**. After each pitch, the umpire indicates the count with his fingers; it's always the right hand for balls and the left for strikes.

In giving the count, balls are listed first, strikes second. A count of "1-0" (never say "zero" in baseball; it's "oh" or "nothing") means one ball and no strikes. An "0-2" ("oh-two" or "nothing-two") count is no balls and two strikes, and so on. A **full count**, the biggest there can be, is "3-2," as in three balls and two strikes.

In terms of the score, you always give the bigger number first. (Remember to drop the word "zero" from your game-day vocabulary.) If the home team has two runs and the visitors have eight, the score is "8-2." If the home team has two runs and the visitors don't have any, it's "2-0," said "two-nothing" or "two-oh."

Okay, let's go back to the hitters for a minute. Most bat left-handed or right-handed, but a small percentage of players, known as **switch-hitters**, can bat either way, depending on the pitcher. (Yes, baseball is where that term originated!) Lefties generally have trouble hitting off a left-handed pitcher; the same holds true for right-handed batters facing a right-handed pitcher. So a switch-hitter would hit left-handed against a right-handed pitcher and right-handed against a left-handed pitcher. Mickey Mantle was probably the most famous switch-hitter of all time.

Certain ballparks, those built with shorter distances from home plate to the right-field wall, favor left-handed batters. The Ballpark in Arlington (home of the Texas Rangers and site of many long evenings for this gal) as well as Yankee Stadium boast so-called "short porches," which are lefty-friendly. The short left field in Houston's Minute Maid Park gives the advantage to right-handed hitters.

All batters love driving balls into what's known as the **gap**. Every outfield has two gaps: one to the left and one to the right of center field. As the name implies, fielders generally aren't standing in those areas. This means even a runner at first base is likely to score on a ball hit into the gap.

Runners also advance with the **bunt**. In bunting, the hitter tries to hold the bat still, rather than swinging. He moves one hand toward the end of the bat after the pitch is thrown. The hope is that the ball will hit the bat and then roll just a short distance up a baseline. In certain situations, such as a runner on first base with no outs, the pitcher and the rest of the infielders may expect a bunt because in that circumstance it's such an effective way to advance a runner. Bunting with two strikes, however, is very dangerous: a bunted ball that lands out of fair territory is the only foul that counts as a third strike.

Say the eighth-place hitter gets on base with one or no outs in the inning. The manager tells the ninth batter (the weakest one, remember) to bunt, which is just what the pitcher and the other infielders are expecting. When the batter drops down a bunt, the runner on first takes off for second. The third baseman rushes in, grabs the ball, and throws to first. The runner at second is safe but the guy who bunted is out.

That move is called a sacrifice bunt, one of several **sacrifice situations** wherein the guy at bat puts the ball into play knowing he'll probably make an out in order to advance a teammate. If there are already two outs, no hitter will purposefully sacrifice since it would be the third out and end the inning. Obviously.

A sacrifice fly is a different way of achieving something similar. A sacrifice fly is any fly ball, preferably a long one, in which a runner on third scores before a fielder can throw him out. Making the whole maneuver trickier for the offense (the team at bat) is that it's against the rules to leave a base before the fly ball is in a fielder's glove.

In baseball **force situations**, also known as "force outs" or "force plays," a runner has no choice but to advance on a ground ball because another runner is behind him. Two runners cannot occupy the same base. If it's not a force situation, a fielder must tag out the runner—as in physically touch the runner with his baseball-holding glove—before he gets to the base.

Okay, we're almost done. Just focus one more minute and you can flip to the back of the book and read about shopping, Brad Pitt, and some great baseball movies. But first, there is this little matter of **pinch hitting**. The National League loves pinch hitting for the sake of the pitchers; you see less of it in the American League because of the designated hitter.

Say a pitcher's ahead in the eighth inning but as luck would have it, he'll be the first man to bat in the top of the ninth. And this is one of the many pitchers out there who can't hit worth a darn. Since the game's tight and the pitcher is undoubtedly going to make an out, the manager tells him he's done for the day and calls a pinch hitter off the bench to go to the plate instead.

A **pinch runner** replaces a slowpoke late in tight ball games to increase the odds of scoring. Some guys hit a lot better than they run, so at crunch time, managers may dump a lead-foot in favor of his opposite: a guy who isn't so great with a bat but can sprint like an Olympian. Managers also use a pinch runner when the regular guy hurts himself batting or gunning it around the bases.

If a manager uses either a pinch runner or a pinch hitter, the player who was replaced is gone for good. Unlike basketball or football, once someone's taken out of a baseball game, he might as well hit the showers or grab a hot dog: he can't go back in, no matter what.

Cool: Once a player hits the ball, he's no longer the "batter." Now he's known as the "runner."

Cooler: Never say "zero" when talking about the count or score or anything else in baseball; it's always "oh" or "nothing."

Coolest: A "sacrifice" has nothing to do with the fact that you've agreed to watch a game. Instead, it's any play that advances a runner at the cost of the batter.

CHAPTER 3

Don't Let 'Em Score!: The Rules of Defense

You may not remember the advice your mother gave as you fretted over pore visibility and panty lines in the moments preceding your first date, but odds are the words "knees" and "together" were uttered in a single sentence.

Your mom, in effect, was giving you an early lesson in defensive strategies: ways to keep the guy from scoring.

Here's how they do it on the diamond.

In baseball, every element of the defense is geared toward a single goal: preventing anyone on the opposing team from crossing home plate and scoring. For the guys in the field, the faster the batters are out, the better. It's that simple.

A typical game ends when each team makes twenty-seven outs—or three outs per inning for nine innings. But since this is baseball, exceptions abound—two main exceptions in this case.

Baseball games can never end in a tie (the 2002 All-Star Game was a glaring exception). So if neither team has scored or if both sides have the same number of runs after nine innings, they head into extra innings and play until someone wins. Since there are no time limits in baseball, a tied game can continue indefinitely. The longest recorded professional game, a minor-league matchup between the Rochester Red Wings and the Pawtucket Red Sox, started the evening of April 18, 1981. After 32 innings and a score of 2-2, play was suspended at 4 A.M.! The teams finished the game a couple of months later. Total hours played: nearly eight and a half. (A typical game lasts about three hours.)

The top of the inning is the first half when the visitors bat; the bottom of the inning is the second half when the home team takes its turn at the plate. If the visitors are behind after batting at "the top of the ninth," (their last turn at bat and therefore their last chance to score), then the game is over. There's no reason for the home team to hit at the "bottom of the ninth" if they're ahead. After all, they've already won.

The following are the most common ways to make an out:

- Three strikes, called "striking out."
- The batter hits a ground ball, which a fielder catches and throws to base before the runner makes it there and touches the bag.
- A fielder catches a fly ball while it's airborne. The fly may be in fair or foul territory, as long as it winds up in a fielder's glove before hitting the ground.
- The batter is tagged out. This happens when a fielder with the ball inside his glove touches a baserunner before the runner reaches a base.
- Any time a fielder catches a foul ball.
- That pesky Infield Fly Rule: with less than two outs and at least two runners on base, if an umpire believes a pop fly could have been easily caught, the batter is automatically out and the runners advance at their own risk. Umps call the Infield Fly Rule immediately after the ball is in the air. Why? So a fielder won't intentionally drop the ball to give himself an unfair chance to make a double or triple play. (FYI: If you can explain the Infield Fly Rule to the man in your life, you have already learned too

much about baseball!)

- The batter runs outside the baselines and the ump rules he obstructs or interferes with a throw.
- While swinging, the hitter steps outside of the batter's box.
- The batter goes mental and either passes a runner in front of him or darts around the bases backward, as in sprinting off to third instead of first. This has happened.

Now let's return to your first date. No doubt you realized your mom's advice was only one of several defensive strategies. Proximity is another ploy: how close you sat to your date probably sent a powerful signal about what you expected him to do or not do.

Proximity is also a defensive strategy in baseball. When a successful slugger approaches the plate, the manager and coaches of the defensive team, anticipating a hard shot or a long fly, may tell their outfielders to move back toward the wall. If, on the other hand, they suspect a batter will bunt, the first and third basemen may ease themselves closer to home plate (a move called "playing in").

Now, say your pesky little brother is itching to embarrass you in front of your date. Though this is exactly what you're expecting, your psyche starts to splinter under the weight of worrying about what he'll do.

That's precisely the point of the **pickoff**, another defensive move that keeps runners guessing and prevents them from getting a head start to the next base or from stealing a base. With a runner on base, the pitcher interrupts his sequence of pitches to throw the ball there; this happens frequently with a runner on first, rarely with a runner on second, and almost never with a runner on third. Even if the runner returns to the bag before the infielder tags him, the throw to first has kept the runner from getting a big lead to second base. Catchers can also pick off baserunners.

Let's say runners are on second and third with one or no outs in the inning. The next player at bat is a $10-million-a-year slugger. If he hits the ball out of the park, it's a three-run homer. If he walks, it doesn't necessarily hurt the team in the field: after all, first base is open. With every intentional walk, the manager (who tells his pitcher when to intentionally walk a player) is gambling that the next player in the lineup won't do the damage the guy now on first might have done.

The single most important player in terms of defense is the catcher. Like a goalie in hockey, the catcher guards home plate, often body-blocking runners trying to score. In another play called a **pitchout**, the catcher jumps up and moves to one side of the catcher's box. The pitcher throws directly to him, bypassing the batter altogether. Because the catcher doesn't have to leave his crouching position or worry about the hitter, his odds of throwing out a potential base stealer improve.

Everyone's favorite defensive move is the **double play**, dubbed the "twin killing" and "the pitcher's best friend." During a double play, which the shortstop or second baseman often initiate, two runners are out on one batted ball.

The rare **triple play** results in three runners out with a single batted ball. It may happen only a few times in an entire major-league season. If he sees a triple play, it's guaranteed that the boy who took you to the game will talk about it for days.

Cool: For each club, three outs end a half-inning, meaning the team at bat must take the field (and vice versa).

Cooler: Twenty-seven outs (three outs for nine innings) end a game, unless the game goes into extra innings or the home team is winning after the top of the ninth.

Coolest: Never ever ask your man about the Infield Fly Rule. (Someday you'll thank me for saving you from a lecture on baseball's most annoying issue.)

CHAPTER 4

Well-Armed Men:
Princely Pitchers

My secret crush in high school went on to pitch in the big leagues. Smart, gorgeous, a terrific water polo player in addition to his star status on the diamond, Kyle Abbott had it all and ruled our Orange County, California, high school accordingly. On days he pitched, so many of his groupies went to watch that you had to wedge yourself into the bleachers. The fact that he almost always led the team to victory was simply icing on the cake.

As I learned early on from Kyle, the pitcher is the man in baseball. If he's a starter—the guy who takes to the mound the first inning—he feels enormous pressure to perform. He throws 100-plus pitches (when he's got good stuff) and exhausts himself each outing, usually every fifth game. Standing on an elevated "stage" sixty feet, six inches away from home plate, the pitcher is the prince of the diamond, commanding the crowd's respect and even its awe during an outstanding performance. When he's having an off day, however, booing echoes in the air. More than any other player, pitchers know just how fickle fans can be.

Primo pitchers don't just throw fearsome fastballs and mean curveballs; they must think straight, too. The best can recall in an instant what pitch a particular batter usually nails. They put this knowledge to work by sending something different (and hopefully unhittable) their opponent's way.

The last thing a big-league pitcher wants is simply to throw fastballs, even if they blister toward home plate at ferocious speeds. Instead, he varies his pitches in order to keep the hitter guessing. From his perspective, the crucial concepts are movement and control. Movement means the array of angles the baseball takes as it rockets through the air. Control means knowing precisely where the ball will go; it's essential to hitting the strike zone.

Upon returning to the dugout, the pitcher faces another foe—not angry fans, not testy teammates, not a hotheaded manager who's ready to blow. Far less forgiving are the cold, hard numbers that reveal exactly how he did on the mound. The most significant measures of his performance during a given season are the win-loss record and the earned run average, or ERA. To determine a **win-loss record**, the following is taken into account: a starting pitcher qualifies for a win if he works at least five innings and leaves the game with his team ahead. If his teammates lose the lead at any time after he departs, the starter forfeits the win; the loss, however, isn't counted against him in his stats. A twenty-game winning season is very cool.

Since an earned run is any run that scores by virtue of a hit or a walk (and not by an error), an **earned run average**, or **ERA**, equals the number of earned runs a pitcher gives up per nine innings. Sorry to introduce a bit of math here but it can't be helped. To calculate an ERA, multiply the number of earned runs by 9. Divide the result by the number of innings pitched. Say you pitched nine innings and gave up three runs. Multiply 3 by 9, which is 27. Then divide that number (27) by 9. Your ERA is 3.00. If you pitched seven innings and gave up four runs, then you would multiply 4 by 9, which is 36. Then divide 36 by 7, and your ERA equals 5.14. These days, an ERA under 4.00 is considered good; an ERA under 3.00 is superb.

To get those numbers, here's what they pitch:

Fastball

The fastball is the gold standard, the move by which most professional pitchers are measured. A four-seamed fastball, called that because of the way the pitcher holds it, can travel at startling speeds, topping 100 miles per hour. The pitcher's repertoire also includes a two-seamer, which the pitcher holds a little differently than the four-seamer.

The fastball lacks the rotation or change of direction that characterizes other pitches. Nevertheless, it's often the hardest to hit. A cut fastball, or "cutter," is especially tough because it bears down on a hitter's hands.

Split-finger fastball *(Nicknames: splitter, sinker, sinkerball)*

As this sneaky ball arrives at home plate, it dives into the dirt at the last second, meaning it is a "breaking ball," a ball that moves unexpectedly. Split-fingered fastballs are almost impossible to hit; if a batter does manage to grab a piece of it, the ball won't travel far. Pitchers who master the split-fingered fastball earn big bucks.

Curveball *(Nicknames: Uncle Charlie, hooks)*

Until the '40s, almost everyone considered the curveball an optical illusion. But Uncle Charlie is very real—and very hard to hit. ("It's almost like swatting flies," someone once said.) The arched path the pitch takes is a result of the aerodynamic effects of the spinning ball.

Killer curveballs shift direction from where they start, moving away from the hitter after reaching the strike zone. For the pitchers, it's all in the wrist and not necessarily thrown that hard. And while most hitters can tell when this kind of breaking ball is coming toward them, it doesn't guarantee they'll make contact with the bat.

Change-up

This tricky toss succeeds by catching the hitter off-guard. The pitcher's almost frantic windup makes the batter expect a fastball. But since change-ups are a good 10 to 15 miles per hour slower than fastballs, it's almost as if someone put on the emergency brake as the ball nears the plate. The baffled batter swings too early and strike!

Slider

A slider is a fast-moving ball that darts downward, upward, or into the hitter at the last moment. The element of surprise helps make this breaking ball a serious threat.

Knuckleball

Throughout the history of the game, few pitchers have thrown knuckleballs with consistent success. Knuckleballers let the nails of their index and middle finger on their pitching hand grow out so they can dig them into the seams of the baseball (ouch!). Then they put their knuckles onto the ball and let it rip.

Unlike other pitches, the knuckleball has no rotation or movement; it's almost pushed up to the plate, like a shot put. The ball doesn't travel fast, so batters know what's coming. But because the ball constantly changes directions it's almost impossible to hit or catch. In fact, when a knuckleball pitcher is on the mound, catchers use a different mitt, one that's the size of a lampshade.

Screwball

A screwball is a pain to throw, literally: to do it correctly, a pitcher must twist his arm, wrenching his elbow and wrist. But such effort is often rewarded. A screwball has the opposite motion of a curveball. In other words, a right-handed pitcher's screwball will move the same way as a left-handed pitcher's curveball.

So now you know seven different pitches: fastball,

split-finger fastball, curveball, change-up, slider, knuckle-ball, and screwball. Over time you'll come to recognize the nicknames as well. Think of how cool it will be when someone mentions an Uncle Charlie and you know what he's talking about! These balls are what the pitchers throw. Now more about the types of pitchers.

Major League Baseball teams have eleven or twelve pitchers on their roster, more than any other type of player. That's because pitchers fall into distinct categories according to their specific functions on the field. There are four basic types of pitchers in Major League Baseball: starters, relievers, setup men, and closers.

Starters

The team's ace is its top starter, the best of the best. Most clubs have five starters in their rotation, meaning each guy pitches every fifth game, or around thirty-five games a season. On good days, starters go at least six innings. A complete game—pitching all nine innings—has become rather rare.

Relievers

The bullpen, which in this context means all pitchers other than the starter, includes two types of relievers: long relievers and middle relievers.

A long reliever comes into the game quickly if the starter can't cut it that day. Groomed to go several innings, long relievers often pitch from the third to the seventh innings.

Middle relievers usually inherit the ball in the sixth or seventh inning. It's a fairly anonymous position, devoid of much glory. These guys are middlemen whose only goal is to keep the other team from scoring.

Setup Men

Of all the boys in the bullpen, the setup pitcher on average sees the least amount of action. Depending on who will be at bat, the pitching coach will call up either a left-handed or a right-handed setup man, most often in the seventh or eighth inning. As a result, these pitchers often face only one troublesome hitter the entire game.

Closers

More often than not, the fate of a ball game rests on the closer's massive shoulders. He comes into the game at the end to make the last three outs and, hopefully, see his team to victory.

Because of this, the closer must have nerves of steel, a competitive streak that won't quit, and a mercenary mentality. He also must be a little crazy. (Definitely not marriage material for anyone who craves stability in a mate.)

The closer often inherits grave situations, like runners on base or the best of the opponent's offense heading to the plate. And since he's usually only there one inning, the closer's fortunes can turn on a single pitch.

So why do these guys willingly place themselves in such predicaments? First, they're instant heroes if all goes their way. Moreover, they can play every other day or sometimes even daily since they're not throwing many pitches. And finally, most of these guys thrive on snuffing out rallies and sending the other team packing. Think of it as a rush on par with shopping the after-Christmas sales.

Every pitcher dreams about a shutout, a no-hitter, and the ultimate: a perfect game.

A **shutout** means not one single runner scored during a game. The pitcher may have given up nineteen hits and walked a dozen batters, but as long as no one scored, it's a shutout. (You'll also hear it referred to as "whitewashing" or "blanking" the opposing team.)

A **no-hitter** is just as it sounds: not a single batter reached first safely by virtue of a base hit. The pitcher may walk someone. Batters can get on base, and even score, by virtue of errors, sacrifices, or a hit-by-pitch. But there were no hits.

For pitchers, a **perfect game** is the Kentucky Derby, the Superbowl, and Wimbledon all rolled into one. The pitcher faced 27 batters (three per nine innings) and got every one of them out, typically with the help of his teammates in the field. It's an exceptional accomplishment, one that only a handful of pitchers have ever achieved.

Cool: A team's best starting pitcher is known as the ace.

Cooler: A perfect game is when a starting pitcher retires 27 consecutive batters without one of them getting to base. It's the ultimate pitching victory.

Coolest: Stay away from the closer: he's crazed.

CHAPTER 5

Here Comes the Judge: Understanding the Umpire

Most everyone thinks the ump's a grump. He's despised universally, even though he's indispensable to the game. The players decry discrimination, coaches second-guess his calls, and irate packs of fans chant "kill the umpire" at the slightest provocation.

But there's more to the ump than stereotype suggests. As the ultimate arbiters of the sport, umpires rule the diamond by enforcing the game's regulations. They must have an unerring understanding of the game, good eyesight, and a sense of fair play. Plus, they're supposed to remain cool, calm, and objective in the wake of inflamed emotions and overheated exchanges.

Only 64 guys umpire in the major leagues each season. Like the players, most umps have been promoted from the ranks, often after spending years as one of the 180 umpires in the minors. Unlike players, umpires must graduate from one of a handful of accredited schools in the United States. Also unlike plenty of players, they're not making millions; on average umps earn around $100,000 a season.

Just as a courtroom judge ought to be objective, umpires must act impartially in order to keep their credibility within the baseball community. Every game, they make dozens of rapid-fire decisions while enforcing the rules. The most important calls are the following:

- Balls and strikes
- Fair and foul balls
- Calling runners safe or out
- Illegal pitches
- Ejecting managers, coaches, or players

Four umpires stand on the field from the first pitch to the last out. The ump positioned behind home plate (the "home plate umpire") has the toughest job: deciding which pitches fall into the strike zone—calls that translate into balls and strikes. Location makes the home plate ump's duty the most dangerous, too; like the catcher, he puts on plenty of protective padding and "armor," including a mask.

The remaining three umps station themselves near first, second, and third base. During post-season games, two additional field umpires do their thing in left and right field.

Traveling in teams around the country and to the two MLB cities in Canada, the same crew of officials works every game of a three- or four-day series before hopping a plane to the next city. In the regular season, the four umpires working together rotate their positions each game. On the diamond, they use a consistent set of signals to indicate, quickly and accurately, their calls. If you miss the sign, listen for the announcer, who should repeat the ruling.

Here is a rundown of signals for rulings:

Out: The ump makes a "thumb's up" with his right hand to indicate an out.

Safe: He crosses both arms in front of his body in an "X," then moves his arms out straight, parallel to the ground, as if pretending to fly.

Strike: Every ump has his own signature style for calling strikes. Most often, the ump points his index finger with his right hand. If he's a showman, he may also shout "steee-rike!"

Foul: He raises both arms straight overhead, like a football ref calling a touchdown.

Time Out: He extends both arms out like he's making the "Y" in "YMCA."

Ball: The umps don't have a signal for balls.

Since Major League Baseball has no instant replay for the umps to consult, for the most part their rulings stand—right or wrong. Occasionally on close calls, two or more of them huddle to discuss what to do. They can also reverse a decision. Players and managers rarely gain ground by arguing their case, however; when tempers flare, umpires often exercise their right to toss a sassy player or coach from the game. And once an ump says go, his word is law: those ejected from the game can't even sit in the dugout with their teammates.

A lone gutsy gal has come close to umpiring in Major League Baseball. In 1988, after spending six years calling games in the minors, Pam Postema officiated a spring training game between the Yankees and Braves. But despite her reputation for fairness and skill, she never made it to the majors. (She did write a book published in the early '90s called *You've Got to Have Balls to Make It in This League.*)

Today, a handful of feisty females umpire in the minors.

Cool: The ump's main jobs are calling balls and strikes, safe or out, and enforcing civility on the field.

Cooler: Umpires must graduate from an accredited school, then toil in the minor leagues for years, before they can work in the majors.

Coolest: The umpire's word is law . . . even if he's wrong.

CHAPTER 6

Sacred Spaces:
Those Sensational Stadiums

Even a steadfast nonfan is liable to feel impressed and a bit overwhelmed the first time she sets foot inside a major-league ballpark. Whether pristine and new (like San Francisco's Pac Bell Park) or steeped in tradition (à la Fenway in Boston), every "yard" serves as a cathedral of sorts to the sport. The stadiums, quite simply, are cool.

True lovers of baseball can spit out names of the ballparks faster than some of us can reel off the fat contents of our favorite foods. If you aspire to remember the various venues or, for that matter, the teams, begin by breaking down the list into leagues and divisions. Major League Baseball (MLB) has two leagues: The National League (NL), established in 1876, consisting of 16 teams; and the "upstart" American League (AL), founded in 1900, which has 14 teams.

Ostensibly split according to geography, each league is organized into the East, Central, and West Divisions. The club with the best record on the last day of regular season play, which totals 162 games, wins its division. (Uncork the champagne and spray it all over your buddies, boys!)

The three NL pennant winners (one from each division) earn a spot in the playoffs for the division championships. One "wild card" team also participates. The wild card is the club with the next best record in its league, after the division winners. The reason for the wild card is that you need an even number of teams (in this case four) to play in the championship series. The three AL pennant winners (one from each division) also earn a spot in the playoffs, along with a wild card team for their league.

The winners of the National League and the American League Division Championships advance to the World Series, a best-of-seven contest that's scheduled to take place every October.

Other than the World Series, the only times AL and NL teams face each other are preseason matchups and interleague play.

Preseason games are held in either Florida or Arizona—and not just so the guys can work on their tans. That's where all of the teams gather for spring training, a six-week period starting around Valentine's Day intended to whip the players into shape. (Think boot camp for rich guys, with lots of spectators distracting them from their aches and strains.) Up until opening day, which is usually in early April, clubs play exhibition games that don't count in the regular season standings.

Interleague play, which first began in 1996, provides a second opportunity for NL and AL teams to meet and compete. But this time the outcome matters as much as any other game in terms of a team's overall record. Interleague games have proven a hit with the fans, who love seeing crosstown or same-state teams, such as the Chicago White Sox and Cubs or the Florida Marlins and Devil Rays, go head-to-head.

Here's a list of all 30 ballparks, according to the league and division:

The National League

East Division

Atlanta Braves	Turner Field
Florida Marlins	Pro Player Stadium in Miami
Montreal Expos	Olympic Stadium
New York Mets	Shea Stadium in Queens
Philadelphia Phillies	Veterans Stadium

Central Division

Chicago Cubs	Wrigley Field
Cincinnati Reds	Great American Ball Park
Houston Astros	Minute Maid Park
Milwaukee Brewers	Miller Park
Pittsburgh Pirates	PNC Park at North Shore
St. Louis Cardinals	Busch Stadium

West Division

Arizona Diamondbacks	Bank One Ballpark in Phoenix
Colorado Rockies	Coors Field in Denver
Los Angeles Dodgers	Dodger Stadium
San Diego Padres	QualComm Stadium
San Francisco Giants	Pacific Bell Park

The American League

East Division

Baltimore Orioles	Oriole Park at Camden Yards
Boston Red Sox	Fenway Park
New York Yankees	Yankee Stadium in the Bronx
Tampa Bay Devil Rays	Tropicana Field
Toronto Blue Jays	SkyDome

Central Division

Chicago White Sox	Comiskey Park
Cleveland Indians	Jacobs Field

Detroit Tigers	Comerica Park
Kansas City Royals	Kauffman Stadium
Minnesota Twins	Hubert H. Humphrey Metrodome in Minneapolis

West Division

Anaheim Angels	Edison International Field
Oakland Athletics	Oakland-Alameda County Coliseum
Seattle Mariners	SAFECO Field
Texas Rangers	The Ballpark in Arlington

While the dimensions of the infields are the same in every ballpark, other physical factors differ considerably. Though most are still outdoors, the current trend in iffy climates is to build parks with retractable roofs. Also, the lengths and angles of the outfield, back walls, and outer fences relative to home plate are unique in every stadium.

Three-quarters of the parks boast real grass. The drawback of grass is a lack of uniformity—a groundball might hit a knot in the green, sending it in an unexpected direction. Places like the SkyDome and Veterans Stadium have artificial turf. Minimal maintenance is the primary advantage of faux grass. But taking a tumble on the fake flora, which covers a concrete slab, can smart. A lot.

Cool: There are 16 teams in the National League and 14 teams in the American League.

Cooler: The only time NL and AL teams compete are during spring training, interleague games, and the World Series.

Coolest: The stadiums themselves, new or old, are very cool.

CHAPTER 7

Sitting Pretty: The Best
Seats to Buy and Why

Setting your sights on attaining super-wife status by surprising your spouse with season tickets? How about taking your boyfriend or your kids to a game to celebrate a special occasion? Or maybe you are hoping to nab your very own foul ball?

Though all 30 major league baseball stadiums vary in size, shape, and seating configurations, some basic strategies can help you select a spot tailored to your interests.

In general, you can't go wrong situating yourself near home plate. Whether on ground level or in the nosebleed sectors, this corner of the diamond provides an excellent view of the on-field drama between the batter and pitcher.

Sitting along the third base side will give you the best view of the tension and tactics of runners trying to make it home. More than likely, a guy stuck on third is twitching at the prospect of scoring. See him sweat.

If it's exuberant—even rowdy—crowds you're looking for, situate yourself in the so-called cheap seats: the upper decks or the bleachers. Up and over there, it's all altitude and attitude; expect to do the "wave" every few innings and don't be surprised if raucous catcalls and cheers assault your ears. Pack a pair of binoculars for a better glimpse of the on-field action.

Those in search of the ultimate souvenir—a ball from a home run blast—should learn where most dingers land in a specific stadium. In the majority of parks, it's smart to stake out seats near the foul poles, beyond either first or third base. If that's where you're headed, don't forget to bring your glove; otherwise, your immediate future could include broken nails and a bruised palm.

The really chic real estate in the ballpark belongs to the fabled luxury box. Located just above the first tier or grandstand, these pricey suites open up to several rows of seats reserved for the boxes. Businesses often lease the boxes as a perk for their clients and employees.

With luxury suites, you can bask in the comfort of glass-enclosed environs, a decidedly welcome development on a cold, rainy night. Often filled with amenities like a full bar, refrigerator, leather sofas, and big-screen TVs, they may look more like a swanky hotel room than a sporting venue. What chick wouldn't want to spend three or four hours basking in such luxury?

You'll find actual hotel rooms inside the SkyDome. At the Renaissance Toronto, 70 rooms look onto the playing field, a proximity to play that, over the years, has given rise to some interesting situations. More than once, TV cameras have caught couples in compromising positions, giving new meaning to the term "seventh-inning stretch."

Alas, ballpark liaisons aren't limited to Toronto. Several years ago, while one of my best friends and her fiancé were watching a night game between two East Coast teams, a small, flame-red object flew out from the luxury box behind them. Further investigation revealed that the wayward item was a lacey thong.

Cool: Beware of foul balls if you're sitting near first or third base.

Cooler: The upper deck (i.e., the cheap seats) can give you a better overall view of the game's action. Plus, the crowd up there can get a little fun and crazy.

Coolest: A luxury box.

CHAPTER 8

Stop Faking It: Simple Ways to Keep Score

During the six-month season, many a baseball aficionado's day starts with this time-honored ritual: while sipping a cup of coffee, he pores over the box scores in the sports section.

Just what are these cryptic communiqués that intrigue so many of our men? Box scores, found in the daily newspaper or on the Internet, serve as both the official record and the numerical accounting of a given game. They reveal the important elements of every inning, including each player's performance. Unfortunately, they're so heavy on abbreviations as to seem downright mystifying to anyone unfamiliar with the format.

Let's decipher one. First you'll need to know the most common abbreviations:

The Players

p – Pitcher

c – Catcher

1b – First Baseman

2b – Second Baseman

3b – Third Baseman

ss – Shortstop

lf – Left Fielder

rf – Right Fielder

cf – Center Fielder

dh – Designated Hitter

ph – Pinch Hitter

pr – Pinch Runner

Hitting Statistics

2B – Double

3B – Triple

AB – At Bat

AVG – Batting Average

BB – Bases on Balls (Walks)

H – Hits

HR – Home Runs

LOB – Left on Base

R – Runs Scored

RBI – Runs Batted In

SB – Stolen Bases

SO – Strike Outs

Pitching

CG – Complete Games

ER – Earned Runs

ERA – Earned Run Average

IP – Innings Pitched

K/9 – Strikeouts per Nine Innings

L – Losses

W – Wins

Fielding

DP – Double Plays

E – Errors

INN – Innings Played

TP – Triple Plays

All those abbreviations are key to unlocking the meaning of our sample box score, the first part of which is known as the line score.

JUL. 13 FINAL	1	2	3	4	5	6	7	8	9	R	H	E	
NY Yankees	1	7	5	0	0	0	0	0	1	**14**	15	1	◄
Cleveland	0	3	1	0	0	1	0	0	0	5	12	1	

W: <u>Wells</u> (10-5) L: <u>Drese</u> (8-7)

HR: NYY—Posada (16), Soriano (22)

Cle—Gutierrez (3)

This particular line score shows the Yankees scored 14 runs (R), accumulated 15 hits (H), and committed 1 error (E). They scored thirteen of those runs in the first three innings and went on to trounce the Cleveland Indians.

Meanwhile, the Indians had 5 runs (R), 12 hits (H), and 1 error (E). The team scored three runs in the second inning, one run in the third inning, and one run in the sixth inning for a total of five runs.

Yankee David Wells was the winning pitcher; he has 10 wins and 5 losses for the season. The Indians' pitcher, Ryan Drese, went down in flames again: his record for the season is 8 wins and 7 losses.

Finally, three bodacious ballplayers hit homers: Yankees Jorge Posada and Alphonso Soriano, and Indian

Ricky Gutierrez. The numbers listed after each of their names are how many home runs they've hit that season.

Hanging in there? Then let's move on to the true box score, which is what the following information is considered.

NY YANKEES	TODAY							SEASON
	AB	R	H	RBI	BB	SO	LOB	AVG
A. Soriano 2B	6	2	2	4	0	1	1	.313
D. Jeter SS	3	2	1	0	2	0	0	.315
E. Wilson SS	0	0	0	0	0	0	0	.208
J. Giambi DH	4	2	1	0	1	0	0	.318
B. Williams CF	4	1	1	2	1	2	1	.313
R. Ventura 3B	3	2	1	1	2	0	1	.261
J. Posada C	2	3	6	0	0	0	1	.268
J Vander Wal RF	5	0	1	0	0	2	0	.273
R. White LF	5	1	2	0	0	1	2	.261
N. Johnson 1B	5	2	3	1	0	1	1	.239
TOTALS	**40**	**14**	**15**	**14**	**6**	**7**	**7**	

Batting
2B: R Ventura (9, R Drese); J Posada (22, J Westbrook)
HR: A Soriano 2 (22, 1st inning off R Drese 0 on, 0 Out, 2nd inning off R Drese 2 on, 1 Out), J Posada (16, 3rd inning off J Westbrook 3 on, 2 Out)
RBI: A Soriano 4 (56), B Williams (48), R Ventura (63), J Posada 6 (66), N Johnson (42)
2-out RBI: J Posada 4, N Johnson

Baserunning
SB: D Jeter (20, 2nd base off R Drese/E Diaz)

Fielding

E: N Johnson (4, ground ball)

DP: 1 (D Wells-J Posada-N Johnson)

The players are listed according to the batting order. Beside the player's name is the abbreviation for his position. For instance, Alfonso Soriano—the leadoff batter—is the second baseman (2B). Here's what the numbers say he did during the game:

AB: (At Bat) He came to bat six times.

R: (Runs Scored) He scored two runs.

H: (Hits) He got two hits.

RBI: (Runs Batted In) He drove in four runs.

BB: (Bases on Balls) He didn't walk once.

SO: (Strike Outs) He struck out one time.

LOB: (Left on Base) He was stranded on base once, meaning he didn't score.

AVG: (Batting Average) His batting average for the season is .313.

Beneath the columns revealing each player's record for the game are highlights in BATTING, BASERUNNING, and FIELDING.

In the BATTING section, **2B: R Ventura (9, R Drese); J Posada (22, J Westbrook)** means Yankee

Robin Ventura hit his 9th double of the year, this one off pitcher Drese. Jorge Posada had his 22nd double of the year (this time off pitcher Westbrook).

HR: A Soriano 2 (22) tells us that Alphonso Soriano hit two home runs during the game; he's hit a whopping 22 of them during the season. Posada, by contrast, has had 16 homers so far.

RBI: A Soriano 4 (56), B Williams (48) indicates that Soriano batted in four runs during the game; he has 56 Runs Batted In for the season. Bernie Williams, the next player listed, got two Runs Batted In during the game and has 48 at this point in the year, and so on for the other players listed.

As for BASERUNNING, **SB: D Jeter (20, 2nd)** indicates that Yankee Derek Jeter stole his 20th base of the season; this time, he made it safely to second (2nd).

In FIELDING, the Yankees made one error **(E)**. Nick Johnson booted a ground ball for his fourth **(4)** error of the year.

The Yankees also turned one Double Play **(DP)** during the game.

The box score always shows the performance of each team, so decipher Cleveland's grid as you would the Yankees.

CLEVELAND	TODAY						SEASON	
	AB	R	H	RBI	BB	SO	LOB	AVG
C. Magruder RF	5	0	1	1	0	1	1	.242
O. Vizquel SS	4	0	0	0	0	0	0	.282
J. McDonald SS	1	0	0	0	0	0	0	.272
E. Burks DH	.5	0	2	0	0	1	0	.271
J. Thome 1B	4	1	0	0	0	0	0	.273
L. Stevens 1B	1	0	0	0	0	1	0	.115
T. Fryman 3B	4	0	1	0	0	2	1	.228
B. Selby 3B	0	0	0	0	0	0	0	.219
M. Bradley CF	4	1	2	1	0	2	0	.234
R. Gutierrez 2B	4	2	4	2	0	0	0	.266
B. Broussard LF	3	1	1	0	1	0	3	.200
E. Diaz C	4	0	1	1	0	0	0	.211
TOTALS	3	9	5	12	5	1	7	5

Batting
2B: B Broussard (1, D Wells)
HR: R Gutierrez (3, 2nd inning off D Wells 1 on, 1 Out)
RBI: R Gutierrez 2 (18), C Magruder (14), M Bradley (16), E Diaz (13)
2-out RBI: C Magruder, E Diaz

Fielding
E: R Gutierrez (10, bobble)
DP: 2 (O Vizquel-R Gutierrez-J Thome, J Mcdonald-R Gutierrez-L Stevens).

The lone highlight for the Indians was that Ricky Gutierrez went four-for-four, meaning he got on base each of the four times he batted. You can tell this by looking at **AB** (or times at bat), which is 4, and then looking at **H** (or hits), which is also four. (Hits means a player gets on base with a hit. It's only a hit if the batter connects with the ball and makes it on base safely. So if, say, he hits a pop fly and it's caught in the air, it doesn't count as a hit.)

You're almost there, girl! The final grid reveals the game's pitching stats.

NY YANKEES	TODAY								SEASON
	IP	H	R	ER	BB	SO	HR	NP-ST	ERA
D. Wells (W, 10-5)	7	11	5	4	0	3	1	117-81	3.75
M Thurman	2	1	0	0	1	4	0	33-23	6.60
CLEVELAND	TODAY								SEASON
	IP	H	R	ER	BB	SO	HR	NP-ST	ERA
R. Drese (L, 8-7)	1⅓	8	8	8	3	1	2	60-34	6.27
J. Westbrook	4⅔	5	5	5	3	4	1	79-50	9.64
H. Murray	3	2	1	1	0	2	0	47-31	3.37

Batters faced - D Wells 32; M Thurman 8; R Drese 14; J Westbrook 21; H Murray 11
Ground Balls-Fly Balls - D Wells 10-8; M Thurman 1-1; R Drese 0-2; J Westbrook 6-4; H Murray 6-1
Umpires: HP - Phil Cuzzi, 1B - Jerry Crawford, 2B - Joe West, 3B - Brian Gorman
Time: 3:17
Att: 42,631

In the case of Yankee pitcher David Wells:

(W, 10-5):   He won, improving his season record to 10 wins and 5 losses.

IP: He pitched 7 innings.

H: He gave up 11 hits.

R: He allowed 5 runs.

ER: Four of the runs were earned.

BB: He didn't walk any batters.

SO: He struck out three batters.

HR: He gave up one home run.

NP-ST: The NP is the number of pitches or the pitch count; ST is strikes. Wells threw 117 pitches and 81 strikes.

ERA: His Earned Run Average for the season is 3.75.

The rest of the information includes TIME of game (3 hours, 17 minutes) and ATT, the game's paid attendance (42,631 were there).

Congratulations—that's all there is to it. While this new knowledge may never impact your morning routine, look at it this way: though you'd probably rather read your horoscope or Dear Abby instead of the box score, at least now you can if you want to.

Cool: Baseball is a game of numbers.

Cooler: The box score is the game on paper, a detailed accounting that re-creates what happened in a specific game on a specific day.

Coolest: Skip the box score if it makes you crazy. Life's too short.

CHAPTER 9

Don't Forget Protection:
Essential Gear for the Guys

Anyone harboring the notion that baseball isn't a contact sport on par, say, with the ferocity of football or the near sadism of pro rugby need only observe a few choice innings to realize these diamonds are rough.

Sliding at frightening speeds, runners mow down anybody in their path. Outfielders slam into the back wall while racing to catch a blast. Then there's the matter of the baseball itself. At such ferocious speeds, a wayward pitch can inflict some serious suffering if it happens to hit a hapless batter.

Not surprisingly, much of baseball's gear is designed to protect the players. But whether for safety's sake or not, every piece of equipment has evolved since the early days of the game, when a player's glove was not much different than what a regular person would wear on a nippy afternoon.

First Baseman's Mitt

Catcher's Mitt

Baseball Glove

Mitt vs. Glove

Only catchers and first basemen wear mitts, which like their namesake, mittens, have no finger holes. The rest of the roster use gloves that are also made of leather and padding. In this instance, size matters. Outfielders prefer larger gloves to help them catch balls. On the other hand, since shortstops and infielders often need to throw quickly after catching, they opt for smaller models. They can more rapidly pull a ball from a glove that's not too large, often shaving seconds off a throw to the first baseman.

Batting Helmet

First required in the majors during the '50s, batting helmets are made of hard plastic with protective shields over the ear facing the pitcher.

Batting Glove

Some guys wear thin, stretchy gloves on one or both hands to ward off blisters caused by batting.

Catcher's Couture

The inherent risk of a catcher's position means that he is the most heavily protected player on the field. He wears a metal face mask, a chest shield, and shin/knee guards. Collectively, all this gear is known as "the tools of ignorance"—presumably because a bright person would choose to play a less hazardous position.

Ball

Made of horsehide stretched around a thread-covered rubber core and stitched with red yarn, official major-league baseballs are weighed and measured before use in a game. They must be 9 to $9^1/2$ inches around and tip the scales at between 5 and $5^1/4$ ounces. On average, 80 baseballs are used per game. Fans wind up with most of these after the balls are hit into the stands as foul balls or homers.

Bat

MLB rules state that a bat must be wood, round, no more than 42-inches long, and have a diameter that doesn't exceed $2^3/4$ inches. But weights often vary. Some power hitters opt for bats upwards of 40 ounces; others prefer a lighter stick, somewhere in the 34-ounce range. Most bats

are fashioned out of a single chunk of white ash.

Bats used outside the majors and minors are typically made of aluminum, which carries the ball farther and faster. They also don't break, making them a cost-effective alternative to wood. The downside? An aluminum bat doesn't make that nice thwacking sound when it connects with the ball: the metal "ping" can't match the "crack" of the wooden bat.

Cool: Official MLB bats must be no more than 42-inches long and are usually made of white ash.

Cooler: Only catchers and first basemen wear mitts; it's gloves for everyone else.

Coolest: On average, fans wind up with 80 baseballs per game, when the balls are hit into the stands.

CHAPTER 10

Uniformly Appealing:
Clothes Make the Man

Behold the man in uniform.

It's almost a law of nature (like never finding sensational shoes on sale in your size) that any guy becomes much more appealing the instant he dons work wear. Perhaps it's an air of authority he acquires when sporting his on-the-job outfit. Or maybe it's simply that uniforms are conspicuous, crisp, and usually clean.

Like the Marine sergeant or a company of firefighters, baseball players can look downright dashing in their official duds. Sure, their uniforms are designed more to foil rips and stains than to make a fabulous fashion statement. But that doesn't stop many major leaguers from looking downright striking at the start of the game.

It doesn't hurt that baseball's formfitting unis (short for "uniform"; pronounced "you-knees") leave little to the imagination. While their outfits aren't as revealing as, say, a swimmer's Speedo or a sprinter's short-shorts, some players squeeze into the tightest pants possible. It's one way they dress for success: anything baggier might slow them down.

Body-hugging uniforms came into vogue in the 1970s, that all-around unfortunate decade for apparel, which also saw teams turned out in shorts (the White Sox) and eye-shocking color-combos (for a few years, the Astros wore an alarming jumble of orange, black, yellow, and red). The introduction of polyester is largely responsible for the sudden snugness; before the invention of that celebrated synthetic, players wore loose-fitting garments made of pure wool.

At the start of the season, each ballplayer is issued a new working wardrobe that consists of the following:

Jerseys

The at-home jersey has team names on the front while most clubs put players' last names on the back above each man's number. A few teams, like the Red Sox, leave off last names.

The out-of-town or road jersey is gray or a dark color with the name of the city on the front.

Pants

Long pants can be pulled up to the knee, as some do to honor the old Negro League players.

Hose

Sorry to disappoint but these guys aren't struggling into fishnets. Baseball hose are thin white socks that go under the sock/stirrup.

Stirrups/Socks

The stirrup is a knee-high cotton legging that runs over the hose and hooks under the foot. A trendy alternative to the stirrup/hose combo is the two-in-one, a long white sock with black, blue, or red stripes on the inside and outside of the calf. They're designed to resemble the old stirrups. Players lose the hose if they're going with the two-in-one sock.

Shoes

Shoe selection depends on the turf. Spikes are used on grass; for artificial surfaces, teams opt for flatter-soled shoes with small cleats similar to what's worn in football.

As a result of the widespread and lucrative practice of shoe contracts with manufacturing companies, plain black cleats are passé: today's teams showcase everything from multicolored Nikes to crimson Converse high-tops.

Belts

The belt took a hit during the '70s, the heyday of unflattering elasticized waistbands that made even the skinniest players appear to boast beer bellies. Now that a more traditional look is back, teams match their belts to their shoes.

Caps

Remember, never say "hat." MLB teams often boast a multiplicity of caps. Most even have special occasion caps reserved for Sundays and bright green caps worn on St. Patrick's Day. Caps are adorned with the team logo.

Warm-up Jackets

Jackets and pullover slickers aren't just for cold-weather days. Even when it's steamy, the pitcher often sits in the dugout bundled in a jacket as a way of keeping his arm muscles warm and loose.

Sweat and hard play get all of these clothes pretty darn dirty by the end of the game. But no one expects Randy Johnson or Chipper Jones to haul their dirty duds home to their Maytags. After a game, players leave their unis in the care of the clubhouse attendants, or "clubbies." Everything is cleaned in the ballpark's own commercial laundry facilities.

While everyone on a team must wear the same uniform, some members express their individuality through accessories, namely jewelry and hair. Don't expect any Dennis Rodman–style extremes on the diamond, though: team managers are fairly strict about their players' on-field appearance. On game days, the only time you'll glimpse the hipsters dripping in diamonds or gold is during the post-play news conference.

Though team rules regarding jewelry remain stringent, many managers have relaxed their stance on hair. Whereas beards and the like were frowned upon in the '80s and early '90s, today mustaches, goatees, and three-day stubble are commonplace.

What to Wear?

It used to be so simple: the home team would wear white while the visitors were in gray.

Now clubs have closets full of official clothing, worn in countless combinations. The job of choosing the garb for a given game falls to either the starting pitcher or the equipment manager. Home teams must wear white or pinstripes, a favorite among many American League teams. Visitors can be in anything gray or darker.

Major League Baseball's newest teams, such as the Colorado Rockies and the Tampa Bay Devil Rays, enlisted savvy marketers to select consumer-friendly color schemes.

As a result, old standards like red and white have given way to teal, aqua, purple, and tons of black.

The Numbers Game

In the early days of baseball, players were assigned numbers according to batting order: the first man in the lineup wore "1," the second, "2," and so on. Today, players choose their own numbers, usually between 1 and 59.

Two obstacles prevent players from selecting certain numbers. One is if the number has been retired, or permanently set aside in a player's honor. For instance, no Yankee can wear 4, which belonged to Lou Gehrig.

Also, teammates cannot share a number, a situation that over the years has created some tension. Say a superstar who has always worn the number 19 is traded to a team where another player already has that number. Get ready for some serious negotiating.

Players, a famously superstitious lot, have spent small fortunes "persuading" teammates to surrender a shared number. Modest little tokens like Rolexes, BMWs, and cold hard cash often help spur a switch.

Viva La Vintage!

Every season, most MLB teams go back in time to play a game or two with old-fashioned flair.

Fans flock to the ballparks (clearly the point) to see their favorite players in replicas of the wool team uniforms from the 1940s, '50s, and '60s. With the exception of their batting helmets and shoes, the home team and visitors dress in antiquated-looking apparel for turn-back-the-clock days. During these retro games, some teams wear old unis from an "ancestor club"; the Texas Rangers, for example, break out garb that harkens back to the early '60s, when they were the Washington Senators.

Cool: Every player is assigned several uniforms. Dirty uniforms are laundered in the clubhouse after every game.

Cooler: Home teams wear white or pinstripes; visitors wear gray or darker colors.

Coolest: To honor an exceptional player, a club retires his number, meaning no team member can ever again wear a jersey with that number.

CHAPTER 11

What to Wear?: Fashion for the Fans

As women, it's a dilemma that distresses us constantly. What to wear? And if you're going to a baseball game, the stakes can be high: a fashion foible has the potential to overshadow the on-field action, if only for one memorable moment.

Sad to say, sartorial screw-ups at sporting events are far more frequent than fouls. At every game, from Little League to the World Series, you're sure to spy at least one woman in an utterly inappropriate outfit. As many a spectator will attest, there's nothing quite as cringe-worthy as watching a buxom young babe strain to negotiate stadium steps in four-inch stilettos and a skintight mini. While struggling to ascend the stairs, she unwittingly becomes a part of the show.

Avoiding a wardrobe error isn't terribly tricky. Take

heed of the following tips, all of which should help you sit pretty at the park.

Colors Count

What's the biggest gaffe you can make with respect to your game-day garb? Outfitting yourself in the opponent's colors. It's almost a declaration of treason, one worth taking steps to avoid.

The following list should help you avert any colorful catastrophes.

The American League's Hot Hues

East Division

Baltimore Orioles	Orange and black
Boston Red Sox	Red, white, and blue
New York Yankees	Navy, white, and blue
Tampa Bay Devil Rays	Black, blue, and white
Toronto Blue Jays	White, red, and (surprise) blue

Central Division

Chicago White Sox	Black, silver, and white
Cleveland Indians	Red, blue, and silver
Detroit Tigers	Blue and orange
Kansas City Royals	Royal blue and white
Minnesota Twins	Red, white, and blue

West Division

Anaheim Angels	Red and white
Oakland Athletics	Green and gold
Seattle Mariners	Navy, white, and green
Texas Rangers	Red and blue

The National League's Sizzling Shades

East Division

Atlanta Braves	Blue, white, and red
Florida Marlins	Black and teal
Montreal Expos	Blue, white, and red
New York Mets	Orange, black, and blue
Philadelphia Phillies	Red and white

Central Division

Chicago Cubs	Blue and red
Cincinnati Reds	Red, white, and black
Houston Astros	Brick, black, and sand
Milwaukee Brewers	Blue and gold
Pittsburgh Pirates	Black and gold
St. Louis Cardinals	Red, blue, and yellow

West Division

Arizona Diamondbacks	Purple, teal, and copper
Colorado Rockies	Purple, black, and silver
Los Angeles Dodgers	Blue and white

San Diego Padres	Blue and orange
San Francisco Giants	Orange and black

True fans dress from head to toe in their team's colors. Savvy fans also know comfort is critical. And since Major and Minor League Baseball spans three seasons a year, your stadium experience may include anything from sweltering heat to frosty flurries. Checking out the forecast before getting dressed for game day may save you serious misery.

Of course, the bulk of the baseball season falls during the hottest part of the year (hence the "boys of summer"). Most stadiums are outdoors (and the few indoor yards have inferior air conditioning or none at all), so opt for cool cotton clothing. Remember your sunglasses and slather on the sunscreen, paying particular attention to the back of your neck, which always seems to fry first.

Also, wear some kind of cap. Don't fret about hat hair: if your post-game plans require a bare head, simply remove said cap and dampen your fingers with water, then run them through your hair. Lean forward and shake your mane over your head. (This works even if it's short.) Stand straight and proceed to rearrange those luscious locks of yours into a first-class coif. Voilà! You're a vixen once more.

The Purse Police

As you pack your purse, bear in mind the contents will come under public scrutiny courtesy of the newest addition to the stadium staff: the handbag Gestapo.

In recent years, security has grown more stringent at many sporting events. Today, ballpark personnel will inspect your purse at least once as you enter a major-league stadium. The bigger your bag, the longer the look will likely take. Some clubs have gone so far as to ban backpacks and large totes. Other contraband may include umbrellas, beach balls, alcoholic beverages, glass bottles, even video cameras. Check each team's website for a listing of what fans can and cannot carry into stadiums.

Another purse-related warning: ditch the lipstick if you're heading to a game in the heat of the day. Just before a seventh-inning stretch at a Rangers game one August afternoon, I opened a favorite tube only to find it had turned into a shimmering red puddle. Opt for a pot of lipgloss as a sensible alternative.

Seasonal Chic

Unless you're blessed with a luxury box (and a comfy club chair therein), expect to spend a good three hours parked in hard plastic seats. This can be tough on any tush. If the humidity is high and you're wearing shorts, you'll almost surely stick to the seat, and then make that horrible sucking sound when you stand up. Not nice at all.

For comfort's sake, consider hauling a cushion into the ballpark. You're generally permitted to bring any kind of small cushion from home. And most stadium shops sell models that fit squarely into their seating.

Cool: Wear comfortable clothes and shoes to the stadium.

Cooler: Remember proper purse etiquette: leave the big bags at home or risk the wrath of the ballpark's security team.

Coolest: Even if you look like death-on-a-stick in your team's colors, suck it up on game day.

CHAPTER 12

Seventh-Inning Stretch: It All Comes Back to Shopping

We've come full circle: baseball and shopping are indeed inexorably linked.

Each year in the majors, club owners along with select stars split a multimillion-dollar pot generated by licensed merchandise—everything from baseball cards and jerseys to sanctioned team Santa sculptures ("Only two monthly installments of $42!").

So Sammy Sosa gets a few shekels for each poster of him that sells. Team owners, meanwhile, divide the profits generated by all club merchandise, from Blue Jays batting helmets to Cardinals cufflinks. Tapping into the nostalgia trend, MLB teams recently introduced retro items like Brooklyn Dodger uniforms and other old-time team togs. A home run with older fans, this stylized attire also appeals to teens searching for a hip look.

With such big bucks at stake, it should come as no shock that every stadium devotes sizeable acreage to the clubhouse shops. Within these baseball boutiques is a vast array of apparel and objects (think White Sox shot glasses; Marlins magnets; Tigers golf tees). Don't expect to stumble upon many bargains at the ballpark: a single postcard could set you back a couple of bucks.

Encircling stadiums in certain spirited communities are blocks of baseball-oriented shops. In Wrigleyville, the charming section of Chicago surrounding the Cubbies' home field, dozens of stores have turned the neighborhood into something of a baseball bazaar.

Whether you are shopping for baseball items inside the stadium or at the mall, the choices are endless. Teenagers relish video games where they can practice baseball in the world of microprocessors. Younger kids may want a Beanie Baby bear wearing, say, a jersey with Ichiro's name and number. And you'll have no trouble finding infant-sized bonnets, booties, and blankies emblazoned with team logos.

For virtually any baseball-related item, the Internet is also an outstanding source. You can easily bid on collectibles (Babe Ruth Bobblehead dolls, autographed photos), buy authentic equipment, and even order tickets to games. A simple search reveals hundreds of sites for baseball cyber-shopping. Among the best are **www.baseball-store.com**, **www.onlinesports.com**, and **www.lids.com** for caps.

Looking for something sure to be a hit with even a finicky fan? Try a subscription to one of the dozens of baseball newspapers and magazines. Those boasting the biggest circulations include *Baseball America*, *Total Baseball*, *USA Today Baseball Weekly*, *The Sporting News*, *Baseball Digest*, and *Sports Illustrated*.

For anyone trying to score *major* points with her favorite baseball aficionado, an excursion is the way to go. Sure he'd enjoy seeing his team play in another city, but you can do better than that. How about taking him to Cooperstown, a picturesque village 70 miles west of Albany in New York State. This lovely little town houses the temple to our national pastime, the Baseball Hall of Fame.

The centerpiece of the complex is a museum showcasing thousands of "artifacts," from Joe DiMaggio's locker to plaques commemorating every player inducted into the Hall since its inception in the late 1930s. The collection contains some 30,000 objects, including old photos, books, magazines, and newsreels.

Fortunately for you, Cooperstown is a dandy destination, so when you grow weary of all things baseball, simply ditch your fan and head to the shores of Lake Otsego, the Fenimore Art Museum, or the Glimmerglass Opera.

Another option sure to secure the undying gratitude of any baseball buff is fantasy camp.

For one of my husband's landmark birthdays, I surprised him with a trip to the New York Mets camp. That January, Chuck spent five blissful days in Port St. Lucie, Florida, living what he describes as every man's dream: being a big leaguer. He and eighty like-minded guys (plus two fearless females!) fielded pop flies, slogged around the bases, and caroused at the Mets' Spring Training complex, just as Mike Piazza, Roberto Alomar, and the rest of the roster would do a few weeks later.

Most MLB teams sponsor some kind of Dream Week, either in Arizona or Florida (the spring training sites) or on their home fields. Typically, the five-day adventures take place in winter and cost between $3,000 and $4,000. Spouses may attend as long as they ante up for their room and board.

Some clubs, such as the Pacific-loving Padres, take get-togethers to the high seas. During a week-long cruise, shipboard fans can rub elbows with current and past players, test their team knowledge in trivia contests, and have their photos taken with their favorite sports stars.

Several companies host the fantasy camps and cruises, which have steadily gained in popularity since first appearing on the scene in the mid-'80s. The websites of two of the leaders in the field are **www.dreamweek.com** and **www.hihard1.com**.

Cool: Retro chic unis.

Cooler: Sending your fan to fantasy baseball camp or on a trip to Cooperstown. Trust me, he'll spend the rest of his days in your debt.

Coolest: Forgetting about the team merchandise and just watching a game with your guy. That's all he really wants anyway.

CHAPTER 13

Sing It, Sister: "Take Me Out to the Ball Game"

Like much of baseball, the seventh-inning stretch is steeped in tradition. It's a brief lull in the on-field action during which spectators stand and sing "Take Me Out to the Ball Game." Many believe portly President Taft inadvertently started the trend in 1910 when he hoisted his bulk from his seat in the seventh inning and, out of respect, the crowd followed suit.

The famous ditty predates the "stretch." Written by Albert von Tilzer and Jack Norworth in 1908, "Take Me Out to the Ball Game" serves as the anthem of the National Pastime.

Sing it like a seasoned pro:

Take me out to the ball game,
Take me out with the crowd.

Buy me some peanuts and Cracker Jack;
I don't care if I never get back.
So let's root, root, root for the home team
If they don't win it's a shame.
For it's one, two, three strikes you're out
At the old ball game.

CHAPTER 14

Battling the Bulge: Your Ballpark Calorie Counter

From sushi at Safeco Field to Camden Yards' crab cakes, each big-league ballpark offers its own unique smattering of regional cuisine. Certain foods, however, are available in every arena—the peanuts, the hot dogs, the ice-cold brew.

It's nearly impossible to avoid some kind of food and drink during a three-plus hours game. In fact, you could argue that a hallmark of the stadium experience is handing over fistfuls of cash to those exhausted employees who cart everything from soft pretzels to sodas up and down those cement steps.

Unfortunately, most stadium fare is less than conducive to waistline maintenance. So to help you navigate the pitfalls of over-indulgence, here's the Cool Chick's Calorie Counter.

Foods	**Calories**
Nachos – 8 oz.	630
Chili dog	595
Oil-popped popcorn – 5 oz.	488
Jumbo frank with all the fixings	445
Unshelled peanuts – 4 oz.	420
Pizza, pepperoni – 1 slice	347
Pizza, cheese – 1 slice	309
Soft pretzel with mustard	295
Cracker Jacks – 1.5 oz. box	180
Dill pickle – 4-inch spear	8

Beverages (12 oz.)	**Calories**
Pepsi	158
Root Beer	152
Dr. Pepper	150
Coke	144
Sprite	142
Regular Beer	148–162
Light Beer	108–134
Diet soft drinks	0–1

Note: Most franchises restrict fans from bringing coolers into the ballparks. Check each team's website for individual regulations.

CHAPTER 15

Mixed Media: The Best Baseball Websites, Books, and Movies

Websites

For stats, schedules, team transactions, and history-in-the-making, check out the following websites:

www.baseballamerica.com
www.baseballhalloffame.org
www.cnnsi.com
www.espn.com
www.minorleaguebaseball.com
www.mlb.com
www.sportingnews.com

Each big-league ball club also has its own website, which contains diagrams of the stadium, team news, fan forums, and online shopping. Visit www.mlb.com for links and addresses.

Books

Suddenly hooked on The Great Game? Read on, babe.

Baseball As America: Seeing Ourselves Through Our National Game, edited by Curt Smith (National Geographic Society, 2002)

Blue Skies, Green Fields: A Celebration of 50 Major League Baseball Stadiums, by Ira Rosen (Crown, 2001)

Chicken Soup for the Baseball Fan's Soul: 101 Stories of Insight, Inspiration, and Laughter from the World of Baseball, by Mark Donnelly, Mark Victor Hansen, Chrissy Donnelly, and Jack L. Canfield (Health Communications, 2001)

Fair Ball: A Fan's Case for Baseball, by Bob Costas (Broadway Books, 2001)

Fields of Dreams: A Guide to Visiting and Enjoying All 30 Major League Baseball Parks, by Jay Ahuji (Kensington, 2001)

Men at Work, by George Will (Harper Perennial, 1990)

Tim McCarver's Baseball for Brain Surgeons & Other Fans, by Tim McCarver (Villard Books, 1998)

Wait Until Next Year: Summer Afternoons with My Father and Baseball, by Doris Kearns Goodwin (Simon & Schuster, 1998)

The Yogi Book: "I Really Didn't Say Everything I Said!" by Yogi Berra (Workman, 1998)

Movies

When, oh when, will Brad Pitt finally star in a baseball flick? For that, we'd beat the boys to the box office! But until that monumental moment, sink into your sofa for these cinematic spectacles, all of which center around baseball.

The Bad News Bears (1976): A girl [ha!] joins a loser Little League team in this winning comedy starring Tatum O'Neal. (Rated PG/102 minutes)

Bull Durham (1988): Susan Sarandon scores with Kevin Costner in a story about a washed-up pitcher sent back to the minors. (R/108 minutes)

Eight Men Out (1988): John Cusack headlines this fact-based tale of cheating in the 1919 World Series. (PG/119 minutes)

Field of Dreams (1989): An Iowa farmer builds a base-ball diamond in his cornfield and marvels as mystical activities unfold. Back when Kevin Costner was cool. (PG/107 minutes)

A League of Their Own (1992): A fine flick about the All-American Girls' Professional Baseball League that played during World War II. Starring Geena Davis and Tom Hanks. And Madonna. But it's good. Really. (PG/129 minutes)

The Natural (1984): Robert Redford (the Brad Pitt of my mother's generation) struggles to succeed in the big leagues as a 35-year-old rookie with some serious scars. (PG/134 minutes)

The Rookie (2002): Dennis Quaid, who looks better in a pair of jeans than any man has a right to, is everyone's MVP in this sweet but factual flick about a middle-aged high school baseball coach who fulfills his lifelong dream to pitch in the majors. (G/129 minutes)

The Pride of the Yankees (1942): Gary Cooper stars in the story of Yankees great Lou Gehrig, who succumbed to a fatal neurological disorder following a brilliant career. Former teammate Babe Ruth plays himself. Keep the Kleenex close. (NR/127 minutes)

CHAPTER 16

The Name Game: The Cool Chick's Top Ten Players

Tens of thousands of men have stepped up to the plate since Americans first started playing professional baseball in 1846. Hundreds have earned distinction for their remarkable careers, culminating with induction into the Baseball Hall of Fame.

It's no mean feat to whittle down a "best of" list. But after much research, deliberation, and a couple of squabbles with guys who fancy themselves keepers of The Great Game's flame, I gave it a go.

Here is my list of coolest of the cool, listed alphabetically by last name.

Hank Aaron Baseball's best home run hitter, he racked up a whopping 755 dingers in his twenty-three-year career. Played in the '50s, '60s, and '70s for Milwaukee and Atlanta.

Barry Bonds Enjoys the distinction of being the fourth member of the 600 home run club. (Hank Aaron, Babe Ruth, and Bonds' own godfather, Willie Mays, are the only other big leaguers with lifetime home run totals of more than 600.) This San Francisco Giant also holds the single season home run record: in 2001, he hit homers 73 times.

Mickey Mantle Widely reputed as the all-time greatest switch-hitter, Mantle played for the Yankees in the '50s and '60s.

Willie Mays This center fielder played for the New York Giants at the same time Mantle was a Yankee; when the club moved to San Francisco, so did he. Mays was an all-around standout in terms of hitting, fielding, and running.

Cal Ripken, Jr. In 1995, the "Iron Man" surpassed Yankee Lou Gehrig's record of playing 2,130 consecutive games; Ripken ultimately showed up for work as a second baseman for the Orioles 2,632 times without a single absence.

Jackie Robinson In addition to being one of the greatest all-around players in baseball history, Robinson became the first black athlete to play Major League Baseball in the twentieth century. His contract in 1947 to play second baseman for the Brooklyn Dodgers ended years of discrimination in baseball.

Pete Rose Considered Major League Baseball's best batter with a record 4,256 hits during his career—which spanned the '60s, '70s, and '80s—Rose played for the Cincinnati Reds. He was banned from the Baseball Hall of Fame because of gambling.

Babe Ruth His real name is George Herman Ruth and he's the granddaddy of the game. The "Babe" or "Bambino" played for the Red Sox and Yankees the first three decades of the twentieth century. He's considered the best power hitter of all time. Many believe the ill-fated Red Sox still suffer the curse of the Bambino: after trading Ruth to the Yankees, the Red Sox never won a World Series again.

Ted Williams Nicknamed "The Splendid Splinter," Williams is the last big leaguer to hit .400. This legendary Red Sox took time off while at the top of his game to fight in World War II and Korea. He died in 2002.

Cy Young The pitcher with the most wins in the history of the game, Young played from 1890 to 1911 in Boston, Cleveland, and St. Louis. Today, the top pitcher in the American League and National League each season receives the Cy Young Award.

Glossary

Ace: A team's top pitcher.

All-Star Game: Matchup in July between players from the National League and American League. Fans vote for the starting eight on each league's team; managers choose the pitchers and the rest of the lineup. Every club sends at least one guy to the game, which different stadiums host each year.

Assist: A ball thrown from one player to another resulting in an out.

Balk: An illegal move by the pitcher. Among the most common ways to commit a balk is if the pitcher does not pitch to a batter after coming to a complete stop in his windup. Many balks are also committed in the process of attempting a pick-off (see separate glossary entry). On a balk, any runner on base advances one base.

Ball: A ball is the five-ounce, white, horsehide-covered orb used to play the game. A ball is also a pitch out of the strike zone—if it's too high, low, inside, or outside. If four balls are thrown to a batter, he walks to first base.

Base Hit: (Also called "single") A batted ball that takes the hitter safely to first base.

Bases Loaded: Runners on first, second, and third base.

Batter's Box: The rectangular space outlined in chalk parallel to home plate. It's where the hitters stand when at bat.

Batting Average: The number of hits divided by the number of at bats for a given hitter. The higher the number, the better. Any batting average over .300 is considered excellent. Anything under .260 is pretty marginal in the majors. Anything less than .200 is known as "below the Mendoza Line," named after a former major league player who couldn't hit worth squat.

Batting Order: (Also called "lineup") The sequence, assigned by each team's manager before the game starts, in which the players hit during a given game.

Box Score: A series of grids containing all of the data relevant to a game, including the performance of every player who appears in the game.

Breaking Ball: A pitch that suddenly changes direction near home plate. Curveballs, sliders, screwballs, and knuckleballs are all breaking balls—and tough to hit.

Bullpen: The area in which the pitchers (minus the starters) hang out during a game, waiting to see if and when they'll be called to play. It is also a collective term referring to a team's relief pitchers, as in, "Our bullpen blows this year."

Bunt: When the hitter holds the bat parallel to the ground, moving one hand toward the end of the bat (instead of swinging) after the pitch is thrown. He wants to stop the ball with the bat so it won't travel far. A good bunt either puts the batter on first base or advances another runner.

Call: An umpire's decision. Among the most common calls are safe or out; ball or strike; fair or foul.

Cleanup Hitter: The fourth guy in the lineup or batting order. He's a slugger who's counted on to score and to drive in runs.

Closer: A relief pitcher who often finishes the game. It's his job to come in during the ninth inning and get the final three outs.

Count: The combination of balls and strikes during a

given at bat. A 3-1 count means three balls and one strike. Balls are always listed first; strikes second.

Designated Hitter: The player who does nothing else but bat in place of the pitcher. Only the American League has a designated hitter or DH.

Diamond: The entire playing field, divided into the infield and outfield.

Disabled List: Players are put on the DL when an injury prevents them from being on their team's 25-man active roster.

Division: Teams in both leagues are separated into three divisions: East, Central, and West. The top finishers from each division (plus a Wild Card team with the next best record) go to the playoffs.

Dinger: (Also called "blast," "four-bagger," "tater," "going yard," and "homer") A home run.

Double: A hit that takes the batter to second base.

Doubleheader: Two games played back-to-back the same day by the same teams.

Double Play: (Also called "twin killing" or "the pitcher's best friend") Two outs with one batted ball.

Dugout: Areas along the first and third baselines where members of each team hang out during a game when they're not on the field. The dugout alongside the third baseline is generally reserved for the visiting team.

Error: A blunder by any of the nine guys in the field that results in the batter reaching a base or a runner advancing when he should have been out.

Extra Innings: When a tie or no score means a game must continue beyond the ninth inning. Sigh.

Fly Ball: A ball hit high into the air that's usually easy to catch. A "pop fly" is a fly ball that stays within the infield.

Foul Ball: Any ball hit outside the foul lines; a foul cannot be the third strike unless it's a bunt.

Foul Poles: Two vertical poles located in left and right field that mark what's fair and what's foul. Any ball that lands on the playing field's side of the poles or hits the poles counts as fair; anything outside or beyond is foul.

Full Count: Three balls and two strikes.

Grand Slam: A home run hit with the bases loaded.

Hit by Pitch: If the guy at bat is struck by a ball, he advances to first base.

Infield: The portion of the playing field that includes all four bases.

Inning: A specified amount of play time consisting of six outs (the first three for the visitors; the second three for the home team). Each ball game has a minimum of nine innings.

Leadoff hitter: The first guy in the lineup.

League: There are two leagues in Major League Baseball: the National League (16 teams) and the American League (14 teams).

No-Hitter: When none of the batters get a hit off the pitcher that puts them on base but someone's walked or there's been an error that sends the batter to first, thereby ruining a perfect game (see separate glossary entry).

On-Deck Circle: The area near home plate where the next-up batter waits his turn at bat.

Out: Any time a hitter or runner is taken out of immediate play. Three outs for each team ends an inning.

Outfield: The expansive area beyond the infield; separated into left field, center field, and right field.

Perfect Game: A starting pitcher retires twenty-seven

batters without a single one of them getting on base. It's the ultimate pitching triumph.

Pinch Hitter: A substitute for a regular batter.

Pinch Runner: A player who takes the place of a runner that reached base. Pinch runners often go in because of injury to the batter or to replace a slowpoke.

Pick-off: A pitcher or catcher interrupts an at-bat sequence to throw to a base. The purpose is to warn the runner not to take a big lead off the base. A runner is picked off if he can't get back to the bag before an infielder tags him out.

Pitchout: A defensive tactic intended to shut down a wannabe base stealer. The pitcher throws a ball to the catcher, who has stepped away from home plate in order to give himself a better shot at throwing out a runner.

Roster: The list of the players on a team.

Seventh-Inning Stretch: During this brief lull in the on-field action between the top and bottom of the seventh inning, spectators at a stadium stand to sing "Take Me Out to the Ball Game." The ritual dates to the early 1900s.

The Show: Another name for the big leagues.

Shutout: When a team doesn't score one single run during an entire game.

Sign: A nonverbal gesture used by managers, coaches, and the catcher to communicate strategies with players on the field.

Standings: The rankings of the individual teams in terms of wins and losses.

Steal: During a pitching sequence, the runner hotfoots it to the next base before the catcher can throw him out.

Strike: Any pitch within the area known as the strike zone that's not hit; it's either swung at and missed or fouled off by the hitter (except when there are already two strikes—a batter can't get the third strike on a foul).

Strike Zone: The invisible area from the batter's knees to the letters on his jersey, the width of home plate. Any pitch outside the strike zone is a ball.

Switch-Hitter: A batter who can hit from either the left side or right side of home plate. He decides which way he'll swing depending on whether the pitcher throws right- or left-handed.

Tag: When a fielder who has the ball inside his glove touches a baserunner to get him out.

Triple: A hit that takes the batter to third base.

Triple Play: A very rare three outs with one batted ball.

Unearned Run: Any runner who scores after getting on base due to a fielder's error.

Walk: If the pitcher throws four balls, the batter automatically advances to first base.

Wild Pitch: When a pitcher throws to the plate in such a way that the catcher cannot field it; runners advance at their own risk because they might be thrown out.

World Series: The winner of the American League Championship Series and the National League Championship Series compete in a best-of-seven series at the end of the season.

The Yard: The ballpark.

ABOUT THE AUTHOR

A graduate of Brown and Northwestern, Lisa Martin lives with her Mets-obsessed husband and their young daughter in Arlington, Texas. She writes about design for *The Dallas Morning News* and several magazines. This is her first book.

ABOUT THE ILLUSTRATOR

Sheryl Dickert received her degree in graphic design from the University of Utah. She has worked as a freelance illustrator for many clients, including Xerox, Starbucks, and Macy's of New York. She lives in Salt Lake City.